Where Is Air?

Where Is Air?
Copyright © 2024 by Sue Ann Matinkhah

Published in the United States of America
Library of Congress Control Number: 2024902365
ISBN   Paperback: 979-8-89091-541-2
ISBN   eBook: 979-8-89091-542-9

All rights reserved. No part of this publication may be reproduced, stored in a retrieval system or transmitted in any way by any means, electronic, mechanical, photocopy, recording or otherwise without the prior permission of the author except as provided by USA copyright law.

The opinions expressed by the author are not necessarily those of ReadersMagnet, LLC.

ReadersMagnet, LLC
10620 Treena Street, Suite 230 | San Diego, California, 92131 USA
1.619. 354. 2643 | www.readersmagnet.com

Book design copyright © 2024 by ReadersMagnet, LLC. All rights reserved.

Cover design by Ericka Obando
Interior design by Dorothy Lee

Where Is Air?

Sue Anne Matinkhah

Air is around us everywhere but what is air? Air is 78% nitrogen and 21% oxygen. Air has lesser amounts of other gases, like carbon dioxide neon and hydrogen and you usually cannot see the air.

When you can see the air, it is probably some kind of pollution. Pollution happens when there is something like dirt, smoke, car exhaust in the air making the air dirty.

Wind is just the air around you moving. What makes the air move? The cold and hot balance in the atmosphere is off. The atmosphere always wants to be in balance. When one area of the atmosphere is heated by the sun more than another it will start to rise and cold air will sink, they run into each other, so the atmosphere is trying to fix itself.

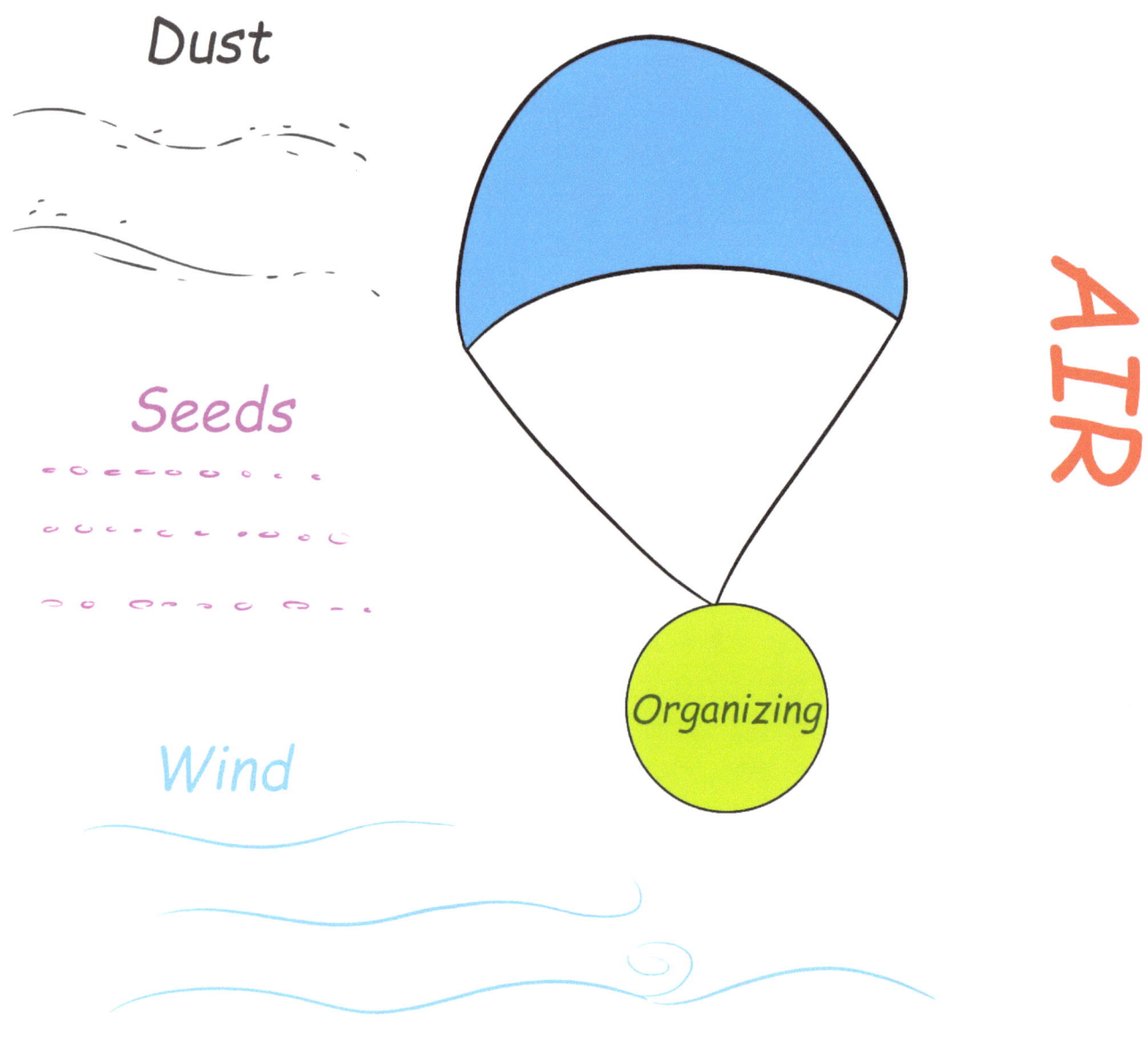

Wind can blow as fast as 253 miles per hour and can carry things for many miles.

Lots of living things live in dirt and water and some living organisms move around in the air. They are called bioaerosols. These tiny living partials cannot fly but they can travel a long way through the air. They travel with help from wind, rain and even blowing or sneezing.

Air pollution comes from:

1. mobile sources by things like cars and planes.
2. stationary sources like factories and power plants.
3. area sources like cities
4. natural sources like wildfires and volcanoes.
Can you think of something that causes air pollution?

Carbon Dioxide is the biggest contributor to human caused global warming. People and animals' breath in oxygen from the air and breath out carbon dioxide. On the other hand,

plants and trees breathe in carbon dioxide with help from the sun because that is what they need to live and then they breath out oxygen.

It is a perfect match made in nature.

Can you think of something to do to help the air stay clean? Plant some trees and watch them grow.

We are lucky to have an atmosphere that has air for us to breath. The air in our atmosphere works like a blanket around the Earth. It keeps our Earth from getting hot or too cold. There is a gas the blanket around the Earth called Ozone that protects us from the sunlight.

Air in the atmosphere protects us from meteoroids that contact our atmosphere. Meteoroids are the matter that floats around in outer space. It can be large or small. When these meteoroids contact our air, they usually burn up before they reach the Earth but sometimes the meteoroids get through the atmosphere protection and land on Earth. These rocks are called meteorites. When we see them in the night sky, they are called shooting stars.

Hoba The worlds Largest Meteorite

The largest meteorite weighs 60 tons and is estimated to be between 190 million and 410 million years old. It has never been moved from where it fell.

Layers of the Atmosphere

Exophere	Space Ships
Exobase	
Thermosphere	Satelites
Karmanline is where outer space starts	
Mesosphere	Meteors
Stratosphere	
Ozone layer protects us like a blanket	
Troposphere is the lowest layer of atmosphere on earth. It is where we can live because it provides oxygen that we can breath, keeps Earth at a livable temperature.	

Air pushes down on the Earth's surface and is called air pressure. Air pressure is stronger at the Sea level because the whole atmosphere is pushing down on you. It is lower on top of a mountain because there is less atmosphere pushing down on you.

10620 Treena Street, Suite 230
San Diego, California,
CA 92131 USA
www.readersmagnet.com
1.619.354.2643
Copyright 2024 All Rights Reserved

www.ingramcontent.com/pod-product-compliance
Lightning Source LLC
LaVergne TN
LVHW070445070526
838199LV00036B/693